Crepe Paper Flower
JEWELRY AND HAIR DESIGNS

20 *Beautiful*
PIECES TO MAKE

LAURA FLAVIGNY

STACKPOLE
BOOKS
Essex, Connecticut

22
24
28
3
34
36
42
44
48
50
54
56
60

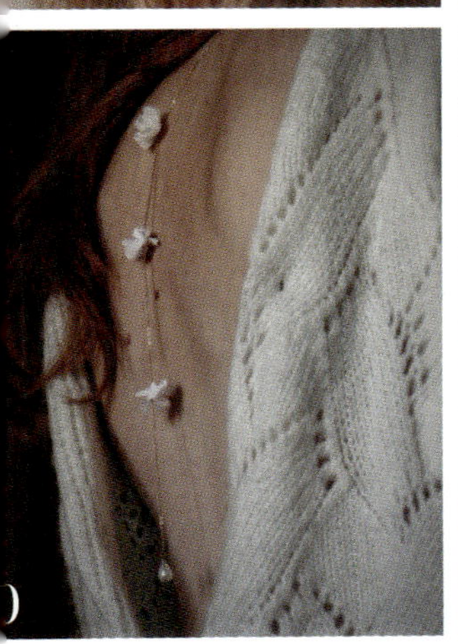

Contents

TECHNIQUES

PROJECTS

-Inspiring Collaborations-

PREFACE

Welcome

to my brand-new book, *Crepe Paper Flower Jewelry and Hair Designs*, in which crepe paper becomes long-lasting flowers that merge seamlessly with your creativity, leading to unique pieces full of personality.

On these pages, I'm delighted to invite you to a new season of inspiration. My aim remains unchanged: to share with you my unwavering passion for paper and the world of flowers, and to motivate you to explore your own creativity. The carefully explained tutorials are designed to inspire and guide you, encouraging you to express your individuality through lovingly crafted jewelry and accessories.

It has been one year since the publication of my very first book (in French), *Jardin Poétique de Papier*, a guide to the art of crafting sustainable, realistic flowers, marking the first anniversary of this exciting adventure at your side.

This first anniversary not only represents a significant milestone in my creative and artistic journey, but also strengthens my determination to share more of my knowledge and encourage others to explore the infinite possibilities offered by paper. Whether it is through sustainable blooms to help decorate your happy events or indoor spaces, as featured in my first book, or through making jewelry and accessories to brighten up your everyday appearance with the book you hold in your hands, I remain driven by a passion to thrive in the craft of paper and flowers. My constant desire is to create, transmit, and spread the joy of artistic expression through this wonderful material.

Today, with this book, I am once again blossoming in the art of imagining, creating, and passing on unique pieces. Here you will find tutorials on how to make lisianthus, cherry blossoms, magnolias, sweet peas, carnations, plants, grasses, Japanese anemones, and more long-lasting and realistic flowers to adorn your jewelry and accessories.

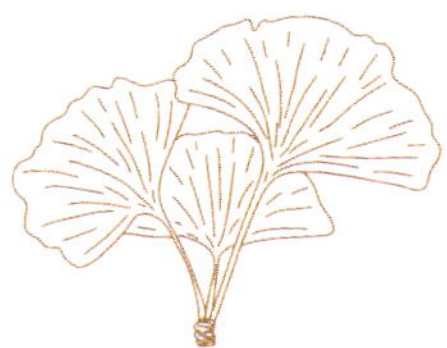

One of the new methods I use in this book that I wanted to share with you is lamination (page 15). This process transforms paper into a versatile material with stability similar to traditional materials while still retaining a distinctive lightness. The paper's delicate grain adds an organic, natural dimension while remaining true to the eco-responsible essence of my creative approach. In this way, my expertise extends beyond floral design, delving into the creation of functional objects that tell a unique story, shaped by the art of paper, inspired by nature.

As you browse through these pages, you will also discover two inspiring collaborations with textile artisans, each with their own ethically responsible perspective: Candice Aubert-Dhô and Sandrina Rocha. The idea of working together was an obvious one, as their art and values have inspired me on a daily basis for many years. They will share with you some of their expertise, highlighting natural dyeing and artisanal weaving.

With this book, my hope is to inspire people to proudly wear pieces that make them feel beautiful and strong.

My hope is that these creations will accentuate your originality and celebrate your differences as you adapt the tutorials to your own tastes. May they be a source of endless inspiration for all those who aspire to express their individuality through unique jewelry and accessories, full of meaning and beauty.

Jewelry has the power to be this one little thing that can make you feel unique.

–Jennie Kwon

ABOUT THE AUTHOR

I'm Laura Flavigny, paper florist artisan and founder of Miluccia Atypical Flowers. My entrepreneurial journey was gently hatched in 2017. Driven by the desire to pay homage to my love of Corsica and my daughter, both boundless sources of creativity, I named my company Miluccia, meaning "My little Mila" on the Isle of Beauty.

"Create doubt for a moment"— that's my philosophy

Inspired by the nature that surrounds us, and motivated by sentiment, I create long-lasting paper flowers that give the illusion of real specimens. I put my know-how to work for you, mainly to create durable, original, and ethical flowers for your happy life events.

During a wedding celebration, flowers become the silent narrators of your story, accompanying you, cherishing you. Nothing can match the significance of a bridal bouquet, which will remain intact forever, a means of holding on to your precious memories of this moment.

Each floral arrangement is meticulously, patiently, and passionately handcrafted in my Bordeaux workshop. My raw material, FSC-certified crepe paper, enables me to give life to the ephemeral, making it eternal. Behind this invitation to dreaming and to freshness lies an ethical and sustainable approach. My flowers will accompany you through the seasons and through the years.

Passing on what I've learned is now an essential part of my daily life. I invest in exciting projects in collaboration with my publishing company, while offering workshops and introductory courses in the art of paper flowers, thereby fashioning creative interludes conducive to artistic blossoming.

Florally yours,
Laura Flavigny

DISCOVER

MY WORK
WEBSITE: www.miluccia.shop
INSTAGRAM: @miluccia.shop

ACKNOWLEDGMENTS

Thank you

To Viviane, my editor, and to Marine, my communications manager, I would like to express my sincere gratitude for your renewed confidence. Your support is an invaluable source of inspiration and a driving force for my well-being, both on a human and professional level. Your commitment to craftsmanship and creativity represents for me a precious opportunity to work with a publishing house like Éditions de Saxe, and I am deeply grateful for these enriching shared adventures. Thank you for believing in me, again and again.

Thank you to my Miluccia, to my family and friends, to my favorite redhead, and to Salma for your unfailing support and love. Your constant encouragement from the beginning has guided me every step of my entrepreneurial adventure.

To my two exceptional collaborators, Candice Aubert-Dhô and Sandrina Rocha, your talent, creativity, and commitment have enriched this book in ways I could never have imagined on my own. To have you by my side in this second book is a real privilege.

Finally, to you, my valued community of readers, I wish to express my deepest gratitude for your invaluable support. Your sharing and your gratifying words have contributed significantly to the success of my first book, a success rooted in the commitment and benevolence of readers like you.

This second book is dedicated to you who hold my book in your hands, you who contribute to the daily evolution of my craft business and my passion for sharing it, making these aspects of my life grow a little more each day.

—Laura

Jewelry has the power to transform an ordinary moment into something extraordinary, revealing your true essence.

–Elizabeth Taylor

Anatomy of a Flower

Botanical Vocabulary

Pistil

The female reproductive organ at the heart of the flower. It is made up of the ***stigma***, the sticky part of the pistil from which the pollen is harvested; the ***style***, the stalk that supports the stigma; and also the ***ovary***, which contains the ***ovules***, from which the seeds are born.

Stamen

The male reproductive organ, consisting of the ***anther***, at its apex; the flower's pollen sac; and the ***filament***, the thin stalk that supports the anther.

Petal

The visible floral part that surrounds the reproductive system. The set of petals is called the ***corolla*** and surrounds the base of a flower.

Calyx

The set of ***sepals***, the sturdier, greener outer stalks of the flower, which surround the ***flower bud***.

Peduncle

The part commonly known as the ***stem***.

Tools and Materials

Here is a list of the materials I use daily to make my flowers and which you will find useful for creating the designs found in this book.

1. Scissors
2. Precision tweezers
3. Wire cutters, round-nose pliers, needle-nose pliers
4. Ruler
5. Wooden pick
6. Hot glue gun
7. White craft glue
8. Decoupage sealer, glue, and finish
9. Thin aluminum wire
10. Flexible wire
11. Stem wire
12. Floral tape
13. Wire
14. Needle
15. Foam brush
16. Artist brushes
17. PanPastels
18. Felt-tip pens
19. Dry pastels
20. Watercolors
21. Artificial stamens
22. A substitute for PanPastels: makeup
23. Jump rings
24. Creole ear wires
25. Fishhook ear wires
26. Teardrop hoops
27. Kidney earring hooks
28. Ear studs
29. Butterfly earring backs
30. Pin backs
31. Cuff bracelet blank
32. Wire choker blank
33. Fine-link chain
34. Flat ring blanks
35. Bobby pins with round blank
36. Bun hairpins
37. Headband base
38. Crimp beads
39. Beads
40. Decorative charms and pendants
41. Decorative cabochons

38
31
23
24
39
25
30
32
34
29
33
40
26
27
35
37
41
28
36

Paper

Crepe paper takes center stage. It will forever remain a real favorite!

To create my paper flowers, I mainly use 60/90-gram paper, which replicates the lightness of a petal due to its transparency and feels delicate to the touch because of its fine texture or veining. I use 140/180-gram paper when I want to enhance the effect of a petal for a more visible grain.

For the tutorials in this book, I have mainly used 60/90-gram crepe paper for the tutorials on jewelry and accessories with long-lasting, realistic flowers. For the tutorials where you'll need to laminate and stiffen crepe paper, I have used 140/180-gram paper.

Depending on the characteristics of your paper, feel free to adjust any stretching steps, as a 60/90-gram crepe paper will not stretch in the same way as a 140/180-gram paper.

We should be as environmentally conscious as possible when selecting paper. An FSC label guarantees that the paper has been produced respecting the protection of biodiversity and its regeneration, demonstrating a core respect for all human beings.

TECHNIQUES

Transforming crepe paper into a firm material with an organic, natural appearance

Follow these steps to laminate and stiffen your crepe paper, using the paper's fine grain to help create an organic, natural effect, while retaining a distinctive lightness that will enable you to create and imagine a wide range of jewelry and accessories.

- *Materials* -

Crepe paper: your choice of colors
Decoupage glue or white craft glue | Foam brush applicator
Clean, flat work surface | Dry cloth

1

First, stretch the paper to soften the grain. Hold the ends of a strip of paper in the palms of your hands and stretch until you feel some slight tension, then smooth out the paper on a flat surface.

2

Once you've cut the pieces to the desired size for your project, use a foam brush to apply the glue to the entire surface of the paper, making sure the glue is evenly distributed.

3

Stack the layers, placing another piece of crepe paper on top of the first, making sure to align the edges and placing the grain of the paper in the same direction. Repeat this step until you have the desired number of layers, smoothing with a dry cloth gently between each layer.

Leave the paper to dry. It may take a few hours, depending on the thickness.

A WORD FROM THE AUTHOR

In this process, crepe paper soaked in glue can present a risk of significant discoloration with certain colors. Always use a protected work surface to avoid any risk of staining your DIY space, and consider wearing gloves.

TECHNIQUES

Techniques in the art of crafting *long-lasting, realistic flowers* from paper

Stamen Filaments

Creating fringe to make the stamen filaments

It is true that this step may take some practice, but don't be discouraged. With a little patience, your stamens will become thinner and more even.

When cutting your fringe, always stop a half inch or so from the edge of the paper strip. This uncut side will enable you to attach the stamens to your stem wire and then have a base for gluing on your petals.

Technique used for the Floral Cuff tutorial in collaboration with Sandrina Rocha, as well as the Magnolia Hairpins and the Japanese Anemone Flower Bracelet tutorials.

Double the paper

I double my paper when I want to make stamens thicker than the weight of the paper I'm using. To do this, gently stretch two strips of paper until you feel a slight tension, then glue them together with white craft glue using a foam applicator brush, smooth with a dry cloth, and trim any uneven edges.

Let dry, then cut out the stamens when needed.

Technique used for the Magnolia Hairpins tutorial.

TIP

To help cut fringe an even width, you can use the width of an edge of a blade of scissors as a visual reference.

TECHNIQUES

Stamen Anthers

1

To represent the anthers, you can color your paper using felt-tip pens, watercolors, paint, etc. Do this step before cutting out the stamens.

Technique used for the Floral Cuff tutorial in collaboration with Sandrina Rocha, as well as the Japanese Anemone Flower Bracelet tutorial.

2

You can also use artificial cotton thread stamens with anthers. They can be found in many craft stores.

Technique used for the Cherry Blossom Earrings tutorial and the Lisianthus Necklace.

3

You can also line the edge of your paper with an additional layer to create anthers that are thicker than their filaments.

Technique used for the Japanese Anemone Flower Bracelet tutorial.

Attaching the Stamens

When you cut your stamens, always leave an uncut edge along the strip. Start with a dot of hot glue on one end of the cut strip and attach the stamen strip to the stem. Apply craft glue to the uncut part and start winding. It is important to maintain the same position and to apply slight tension as you wind. For added strength, once the stamen strip is wrapped around the stem, cover the flat part with hot glue. As it sets, the glue will hold the strip to the stem, so there's no risk of the two pieces coming apart.

TECHNIQUES

Petals

1
Stretching the Crepe Paper

To stretch crepe paper, hold the ends of a strip of paper in the palms of your hands and stretch until you feel some slight tension, then smooth out your paper on a flat surface. This allows you to play with the transparency or to soften the grain of the paper. The stretch will be different depending on the weight of the paper used.

* Stretching crepe paper: **a.** 60 gr | **b.** 90 gr | **c.** 140 gr

2
Cutting

On the templates, you'll find two lines showing you how to position them in line with the grain of the paper. When cutting, hold the template firmly on the paper with your thumb on the front and index finger on the back. Always cut as close as possible to the template, petal by petal, at first. Then, with practice, you'll be able to cut more petals by cutting through several layers of paper.

3
Cupping and Shaping

To shape your petals, your best tools will be your hands and fingers. Gently apply pressure with both hands, positioning your thumbs on the front and index fingers at the back of the petal, stretching the edges outward, while exerting pressure with your thumbs to form a concave shape at the center of the petal. The curve will vary depending on the weight of the paper and how deeply you want to cup or stretch the petal.

TECHNIQUES

Covering the Calyx and the Stem

1 Covering the Calyx

First, to finish your flower, you will need to cover the base to which your petals are glued. To do this, cut a rectangle from previously stretched paper and attach it with hot glue, half on the base of the petals, half on the stem. You can also cover the calyx of the flowers with sepals.

2 Covering the Stem

To cover the stem wire, take a strip of pre-stretched crepe paper, in the width and length you prefer. Attach one end horizontally to the base of the calyx, spread a small amount of liquid glue over the whole strip, then hold it at an angle and gently turn the stem to wind the paper down around the stem. All that's left to do is cut off any excess stem wire.

The Meaning of

Sweet peas

Sweet peas symbolize delicacy, tenderness, and remembrance.

Magnolia

The magnolia is often associated with dignity, perseverance, and nobility.

Cherry blossoms

Cherry blossoms are often associated with fleeting beauty and the fragility of life.

Carnation

Carnations are associated with love, admiration, and fascination, and pink carnations are often connected to maternal love.

Pansy

Pansies are often associated with reflection, consideration, and remembrance.

Peony

The peony is often considered as a flower that represents feminine elegance and beauty. Its lush appearance and soft petals are associated with femininity and grace.

Lisianthus

Lisianthus is often associated with appreciation and gratitude. It expresses the feeling of recognizing the beauty and goodness of another person.

Japanese anemone

The Japanese anemone is often associated with positivity and the anticipation of good things to come. It symbolizes hope and good fortune for the future.

Projects

Half Flower Lever-Back

- Materials -

Crepe paper: ocher

Scissors | Foam brush | White craft glue

Extra-strength glue | Decorative cabochon | Lever-back earrings with flat round setting

1 For this tutorial, start by laminating the paper (see page 15). For this design, use the crepe paper to create a paper that is six sheets thick.

2

Using the template on page 94, cut out six petals.

3

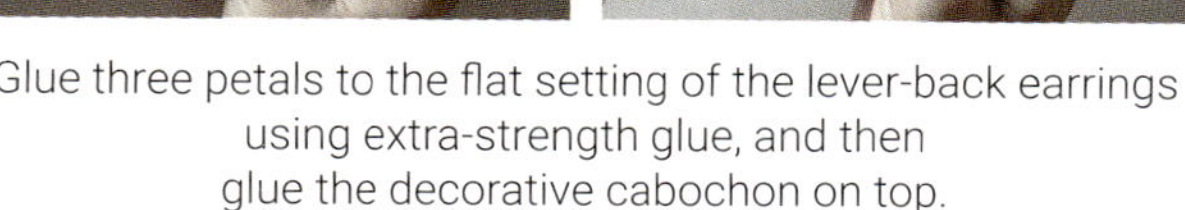

Glue three petals to the flat setting of the lever-back earrings using extra-strength glue, and then glue the decorative cabochon on top.

TIP

Let your inspiration guide you in your choice of color. Feel free to reduce or enlarge the size of the template to create a pair of earrings that is just right for you.

Carnation Pin

- Materials -

Crepe paper:
light pink, green

Scissors | White craft glue | Hot glue gun
Stem wire | Wire cutters | Wire | Felt-tip pen | 1 pin back

1

Cut two strips of crepe paper 20" x 1½" (50 x 4 cm) wide from the crepe paper. Stretch the paper until you feel a slight tension.
For each strip: Fold the strip over several times to obtain a rectangle to fit the size of the template on page 94. Then cut out the strip of petals using the template.

2

For each strip: Don't unfold the strip right away; first cut small points at the top of the petals. You can also use pinking shears for this.

3

Using a felt-tip pen in a shade darker than the selected paper, color the edges of the tips. Then, lightly curve the top of the petals with your fingers.

4

Attach one end of your first strip to a stem wire with a dot of hot glue and roll up the first petal tightly.

5

Place a dot of white craft glue at the bottom of each petal and roll the strip onto the stem, keeping it at the same position and not moving it lower on the stem wire. Wrap so it looks airy and a little crinkled. Wrap the second strip in the same way as the first one.

6

To create the convex part of the carnation's calyx, tie and tighten a wire above the calyx.

7

Cover the calyx with a piece of green paper coated with craft glue, previously cut with points along the edge, half on the calyx and half on the stem wire. Cut out thin sepals as shown in the photo and glue them to the underside of the calyx.

8

Using a strip of previously stretched paper ⅜" (1 cm) wide and cut to fit the length of the stem, attach one end to the base of the calyx horizontally, applying a small amount of craft glue over the entire strip, then hold it at an angle, turning the stem slowly as you as you wind the strip down.

- Assembly -

Make as many carnations as you wish to create a brooch, possibly varying the size and shape of your flowers. Tie several carnations together with a strip of crepe paper or floral tape, cut the stem wires to the desired length, and attach to a pin back. Add some dried flowers to your arrangement if the inspiration hits you!

Ginkgo Dangle Earrings

- Materials -

Crepe paper: blue

Scissors | Wire cutters | Needle-nose pliers | Round-nose pliers
Needle | Foam brush | White craft glue
2 ball post earrings with loop | 2 butterfly earring backs for posts
4 jump rings | Fine-link chain | 2 decorative charms

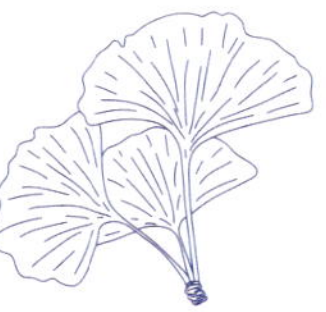

1

For this tutorial, first laminate the paper (see page 15). To create this project, prepare a piece of crepe paper that is six layers thick.

2

Using the template on page 94, cut out two ginkgo leaves. If you have a paper cutting machine such as a Sizzix Big Shot, feel free to use that and vary the shapes.

3

Using a needle, make a hole in each ginkgo leaf where indicated on the template. Then, with a wire cutter, cut two pieces of chain to the length you prefer.

With the needle-nose pliers and the round-nose pliers, open a jump ring and put it through the hole in the ginkgo leaf. Before closing the ring, insert one end of the chain and the decorative charm.

In the same way, open a jump ring and insert it through the loop on your earring post. Also insert the other end of the chain into the ring before closing it to form the loop.

Magnolia Hairpins

- Materials -

Crepe paper:
white, soft green, soft yellow

Scissors | Wire cutters | White craft glue | Hot glue gun | Stem wire
Thin aluminum wire | PanPastel (optional) | Bun hairpins

1

Make one bud at one end of a stem wire using a ⅜" x 5" (1 x 13 cm) strip of paper towel.

2

Cut a ¾" x 2½" (2 x 6 cm) strip of the soft green paper and stretch it lengthwise until you feel a slight tension. Then cut long points on one entire side, leaving about ¼" (0.5 cm) on the other side that is not cut, to be used to make the magnolia's pistils. Separate the strip into two equal pieces.

3

Cut a ¾" x 4" (2 x 10 cm) strip of the soft yellow paper, and stretch it lengthwise until you feel a slight tension. Fold it in half and double the paper by gluing the two parts together, applying white craft glue with a foam brush. Smooth the strip with a dry cloth and let dry. Once the strip of paper is dry, cut a fringe about ⅛" (0.2 cm) long all along one side, leaving ¼" (0.5 cm) on the other side uncut to make the magnolia's stamens.

You can use a PanPastel or a bright yellow felt-tip pen to color the stamens' anthers.

4

Using a dot of hot glue, attach the first strip of soft green pistils around the bud, positioning it as shown in the photo. Wind the entire strip at the same position, and don't bring it down lower on the stem wire. Attach the second strip of soft green pistils in the same manner, just about ⅛" (a few millimeters) below the first one.

5

Using a dot of hot glue, attach the first strip of soft yellow stamens around the green pistils, positioning them about ⅛" (a few millimeters) below. Wind the entire strip at the same position, and don't bring it down lower on the stem wire. Attach the second strip of yellow stamens in the same manner, another ⅛" (a few millimeters) below the first one.

6

Using the templates on page 94, cut out three A petals and five B petals. Pay attention to the direction of the paper's grain when cutting out the petals. The grain of the paper must be vertical to the templates.

You can shade in some colors on the bottom of your petals, front and back, using a PanPastel or watercolor.

7

Slightly shape the eight petals in the same way, top and bottom. To do this, use both hands to gently stretch the edges of the petal. Positioning your thumbs at the front and your index fingers at the back of the petal, stretch the edges outward, while exerting pressure with your thumbs to form a concave shape at the center of the petal.

8

Glue the three A petals with the same spacing between each at a first line along the uncut base of the stamens, using hot glue in the lower, curved part of the petals.

9

Then position and glue the five B petals at a second line, letting your inspiration guide the placement. Cover the magnolia calyx with sepals.

- Assembly -

Cut the magnolia stem to fit the hairpin, and use thin aluminum wire to secure the flower to the hairpin.

A WORD FROM THE AUTHOR

Think about enlarging or reducing the size of the templates to create a set of floral pins with different-sized flowers.

Flower Pin

- Materials -

Crepe paper: your choice of color

Scissors | Needle-nose pliers | Round-nose pliers | Wire cutters
Foam brush | White craft glue | Extra-strength glue
1 flat-pad post earring with loop and earring back
1 jump ring | 1 decorative cabochon | Fine-link chain

1

For this tutorial, first follow the steps to laminate the paper (see page 15). For this pattern, prepare crepe paper that is six layers thick.

2

Once the paper is stiffened and is completely dry, cut out the flower using the template on page 94. Then place a dot of extra-strength glue in the center of the flower and glue on the decorative cabochon.

3

Using the wire cutters, cut six different lengths of chain. Open a jump ring using the needle-nose and round-nose pliers and put the six lengths of chain onto the ring. Before closing the ring, add the flat-pad post through the attached loop.

4

Place a dot of extra-strength glue on the flat pad of the post earring and glue on the flower. Curl up the petals slightly toward the decorative cabochon to give some movement to your flower.

Plant Hat

- Materials -

Crepe paper:
shades of green

Scissors | Stem wire | White craft glue
Hot glue gun | Artist's brush | PanPastels | White felt-tip pen
Floral tape | Hat

Foliage 1

Cut a strip of crepe paper to 4" x 1¼" (10 x 3 cm). Stretch it until you feel slight tension. Along the entire length, cut out a row of teardrop-shaped leaves on little stems, leaving ¼" (0.5 cm) uncut all along the edge of the strip. Then roll the leaves one by one between your fingers. Apply a small amount of white craft glue to the uncut side, attaching one end to a stem wire and winding your leaves around the stem at an angle from top to bottom.

Foliage 2

Cut out a 1½" x 2½" (4 x 6 cm) rectangle. Cut it in half diagonally. On one of the pieces, apply a light line of white craft glue along the diagonal edge so that you can put the two halves together, one on top of the other. You'll need to flip one of the pieces on its reverse side before gluing, so that once the two pieces are joined, the grains of the glued papers form a V. Cover a stem wire with a ⅜" (1 cm) wide strip of stretched green paper previously coated with a little craft glue and attach your stem wire to the back of your foliage. Finally, for the pattern, make dots on the leaves with a white ink felt-tip pen.

Foliage 3

For these leaves, follow the same steps as for Foliage 2, then add shades of color to your leaves using PanPastels. You could also use watercolors, felt-tip pens, makeup, etc.

You might consider tinting your paper with ink beforehand for more shades of color.

Foliage 4

Cut leaf shapes from crepe paper. Using a long strip of stretched green paper ⅜" (1 cm) wide, coated with a little craft glue, attach a leaf to one end of your stem wire. Then alternate placement of your leaves, meaning attach them at different levels from top to bottom along your stem wire. To do this, position your leaf at the desired point and wrap the lower part of your leaf to the stem with your paper strip, making a complete turn. Then wind it down around the stem a bit at an angle, attach a second leaf, and repeat this step until all your leaves are attached to the stem.

Foliage 5

Cut a 4" x 1½" (10 x 4 cm) strip of paper. Stretch it along its entire length. Fold it in half, then cut a pointed fringe, leaving a ¼" (0.5 cm) strip along the other edge uncut. Apply a small amount of white craft glue to the uncut side, attach one end to a stem wire, and wind the strip around the stem at an angle from top to bottom.

Foliage 6

Cut out a 1½" x 2" (4 × 5 cm) rectangle. Fold it in half lengthwise and cut the finest fringe possible on one side, leaving ⅜" (1 cm) on the other edge uncut. Apply a small amount of white craft glue to the uncut side and wrap the strip around one end of a stem wire.

Foliage 7

Cut out a 1½" x 4" (4 × 10 cm) rectangle. Fold it in half widthwise and brush one half with white craft glue. Place a stem wire in the center and fold over the other part of the rectangle. Smooth with a dry cloth, then cut leaves of varying lengths on the two sides of the stem wire.

Cover the stems of your foliage.

To cover your metal stems, take a strip of paper ⅜" (1 cm) wide by about 4" (10 cm) long (length varies according to the length of your stem). Attach one end horizontally at the desired location, apply a small amount of white craft glue to the entire strip, then hold it at an angle and gently wind it downward around the stem.

- Assembly -

Once you've decided on the number of pieces of foliage you'd like to use, create little bouquets by mixing different varieties. Use floral tape to bind them together.

You have several options for attaching these bouquets to your hat. Use hot glue to secure them one at a time or sew the bouquets to your hat, depending on what material the hat is made of.

A WORD FROM THE AUTHOR

Wear your hat proudly on a summer day or simply consider it as a piece of art to decorate your home.

Petal Tassel

Materials

Crepe paper: white

Scissors | Needle-nose pliers | Round-nose pliers | Wire cutters

Thin aluminum wire | 6 3-mm crimp beads

2 kidney earring hooks | 2 jump rings

2 decorative charms | Fine-link chain

Using the templates on page 94, cut out eight petals of each size.

Group together four petals of the same size and place the tips of the petals through one crimp bead, along with a loop made using fine aluminum wire. With flat-nose pliers, crimp the bead, then trim off excess aluminum wire. Make six petal tassels of different sizes in this way.

Cut two pieces of chain to the desired length. Use flat-nosed pliers and round-nosed pliers to open a jump ring. Before closing it, add on the decorative charm and the end of a piece of chain. Do this for both chains and charms.

Assemble your earrings, adding the petal tassels along with the chain and its decorative charm.

Japanese *Anemone* Bracelet

- Materials -

Crepe paper:
soft green, soft yellow, bright yellow, pink

Scissors | Stem wire | White craft glue
Hot glue gun | Paper towel | 1 cuff bracelet blank

1

Form a ball from a 2½" x 3½" (6 × 9 cm) piece of paper towel and attach it to a stem wire. To do this, open the ball slightly, apply a dot of hot glue, slide the wire inside, and round it with your fingers.

2

Cover it with a 1½" (3.5 cm) square of soft green paper previously stretched and coated with craft glue. Pull gently on the edges to make the top as smooth as possible and glue the edges of the paper to the stem wire rod.

3

Cut out a 10" x 1" (25 × 2.5 cm) strip of soft yellow stretched paper, and then a 10" x ¼" (25 × 0.7 cm) strip of bright yellow paper. To create the stamens' anthers, glue half the width of this thin strip along the entire length of the strip of soft yellow paper using white craft glue, and then fold the other half of the thin strip to the back side.

4

Once your paper strip is dry, cut fringe as fine as possible along the entire length, to represent the stamens, leaving ¼" (0.5 cm) along the other edge uncut. This will be used to glue the petals.

5

Use hot glue to attach one end of the stamen strip to the stem wire just below the ball, then apply white craft glue to the uncut part and roll it up completely. Pull gently on the strip to ensure it is rolled up tightly and keep it at the same position on the stem. For extra hold, apply hot glue at the base once the strip is fully wound. Finally, open the stamens slightly using precision tweezers.

6

Using the template on page 95, cut out six A petals and four B petals from the pink paper. If you wish, you can lightly add shades of color to the petals with PanPastels.

7

Give a slightly curved shape to the top of each of the ten petals.

8

Start with a first row of three evenly spaced A petals, gluing them to the uncut part of the stamen strip with a dot of hot glue at the bottom of the petals. Then let your inspiration guide you in gluing the remaining seven petals in second and third rows.

9

Cut out the desired number of sepals to cover the calyx of the Japanese anemone. Bring the bottom of the sepals close together ard curve them up slightly with scissors. Then cut the stem wire below the calyx.

- Assembly -

Make another flower in the same way, if desired. Then, attach the sepals and then the Japanese anemones to your bracelet blank using hot glue.
Finish your composition by adding sepals at the base of each flower's calyx to hide it slightly and give it a nice, finished look.

Energizing Ring

- Materials -

Crepe paper: fuchsia

Scissors | Artist's brush | White craft glue | Extra-strength glue
1 flat ring blank | 1 healing stone bead of your choice

1. Using the template on page 94, cut out several small flowers from previously stretched crepe paper.

2. Glue the flowers one on top of the other in the middle, applying white craft glue with an artist's brush.

3. Place a dot of extra-strength glue on the flat top of your ring and glue your set of flowers to it.

4. In the center of the ring, attach the healing stone bead with extra-strength glue. Finally, close up your flower a little around the bead to give it some movement.

For this tutorial, I have chosen one carnelian bead, which promotes creativity and energy. You can also use one rose quartz bead, which supports self-esteem, or one blue chalcedony bead, which calms anxiety. It's up to you to choose a bead that fits your personality.

Sweet Pea *Hair Comb*

- Materials -

Crepe paper: light blue, green

Scissors | Flexible stem wire | White craft glue | Hot glue gun
Dry pastels (optional) | 1 wood skewer | 1 plain hair comb

1

First, you can use either a brush or sponge to apply dry pastels to the paper to add shades of color to your sweet pea petals. Stretch the crepe paper slightly until it is taut, and then apply dry pastel to the paper and blend with a brush.

2

Cut the desired number of squares to fit the size of the templates on page 95. Split a square in half diagonally. On one of the pieces, put a light line of white craft glue on the diagonal edge, and then join the two halves, one on top of the other. Turn one of the pieces over on its reverse side before gluing, so that the grain of the paper forms a V when the two pieces are joined.

3

Cut out as many A and B petals as needed for the number of flowers you want on your comb. For one sweet pea flower, you'll need one A petal and two B petals. Position your templates with the glue line centered between the two sets of parallel lines. Make small waves with your fingers along the edges of the petals, stretching the paper slightly.

4

Cover your stem wires with a strip of green paper ½" (1 cm) wide, coated from top to bottom with craft glue. Some will be used to make your sweet pea flowers, others to form the tendrils that characterize this climbing plant. To make the tendrils, once the metal stem has been covered, twist it onto a wood skewer to give it the desired shape.

5

With a dot of hot glue, attach two B petals facing each other to a stem wire, leaving the end of the wire slightly protruding. Then glue one A petal to the back of the two B petals.

-Assembly-

Once all the sweet pea flowers and tendrils have been made, cut the stems to the desired length and twist them onto the top edge of the comb. Vary the placement of the flowers, giving them different stem lengths, and space out the tendrils over the entire edge of the comb.

Sweet peas come in a variety of colors: pink, salmon, red, lavender, and more. If you'd like, vary the shades and create unique floral arrangements to suit your own tastes.

Gold Leaf *Hoop Earrings*

- Materials -

Crepe paper: gold

Scissors | Precision tweezers | Foam brush

White craft glue | Extra-strength glue | Miyuki beads | Creole ear wires

For this tutorial, first laminate the paper (see page 15). For this pattern, you will need a thickness of four sheets of crepe paper.

Using the templates on page 95 or your own creativity, cut out the desired number of small leaves.

Thread a few beads onto the creole wire, then, using extra-strength glue, attach a group of leaves, one by one. Leaves made with template A can be placed around the creole wire and those with template B can be placed on top. Thread on a few more beads and follow your inspiration.

TIP

To create your hoop earrings, follow a pattern when placing the beads and leaves for an aesthetically pleasing result. For example: beads – leaves – beads – space – beads – leaves – beads – space – etc.

Mini *Bouquet Pin*

- *Materials* -

Crepe paper:
white, green, violet, soft yellow

Scissors | Stem wire | White craft glue | Hot glue gun
String or ribbon | 1 pin back

Inspiration: Lavender

Cut a 4" x ⅜" (10 x 1 cm) strip. Stretch it until you feel some tension. Fold it in half and then in half again and cut a fringe along its entire length, leaving ¼" (0.5 cm) along the other edge uncut. Divide the strip into several equal parts. Cover a stem wire with a thin strip of green paper coated with craft glue. Wrap one section around the top of the stem wire, then a second a tiny bit below the first, then a third just below that and so on to form a small lavender stem.

Inspiration: Phalaris

Cut a strip 4" long x 2" wide (10 x 5 cm). Stretch it slightly until you feel some tension. Fold it in half lengthwise, then cut a fringe ¾" (2 cm) long on the folded side, leaving ¼" (0.5 cm) uncut along the other edge. Attach the strip to the end of a stem wire, placing a small amount of craft glue on the uncut side, and wind the entire strip around the stem, descending a bit to create the shape of a phalaris.

Inspiration: Baby's Breath

Cut a strip 4" long x ⅜" wide (10 x 1 cm). Stretch it slightly until you feel some tension. Fold it in half and then in half again and cut a fringe as thin as possible along its entire length, leaving half the width uncut. Divide the strip into several equal sections. Cover a stem wire with a thin strip of white paper coated with craft glue. Wrap one section around the top of the stem wire. With the remaining sections create a small bouquet of baby's breath.

Assembly

Make a small bouquet with the desired number of stems of lavender, baby's breath, and phalaris. Gather them together using a strip of paper ⅜" (1 cm) wide coated with craft glue. Attach the pin back with hot glue then wrap some jute or ribbon around the bouquet for a nice final touch.

A WORD FROM THE AUTHOR

Vary the colors and the number of stems to create a mini bouquet that suits you.

Lisianthus Necklace

Materials

Crepe paper:
pale pink, plum, green

Scissors | White craft glue | Hot glue gun | Flexible wire
Artificial stamens | PanPastels (optional) | 1 wire choker blank

1

Stretch your paper until it is just slightly taut to soften its grain. Then, using the template on page 94, cut out the number of petals needed for the amount of lisianthus flowers you want on the necklace.
You will need eight petals for one lisianthus bloom.
Make small waves at the top of the petals as you cut them out.

2

If you wish, you can color the top of the petals with PanPastels, watercolors, or felt-tip pens.

3

Glue the petals together one at a time with a dot of craft glue, overlapping them a bit and creating a slightly rounded line.

4

Attach the artificial stamens to a flexible wire using a strip of paper, previously stretched and coated with craft glue.

5

Position and attach, with a dot of hot glue, the stamens in the center of the petals. Apply a little craft glue to the sides, fold one side toward the stamens, then the second side to form the lisianthus flower.

6

Attach narrow sepals, half to the flower's calyx and half to the flexible wire. Then cover the wire with a strip of paper previously stretched and coated with craft glue.

- Assembly -

Cut the stems to the lengths desired and twist the lisianthus flowers around your choker. Vary the stem lengths as well as the placement and number of flowers.

A WORD FROM THE AUTHOR

You can add lisianthus flower buds to your design. To create a bud, take a strip of paper towel 5" x ⅜" (13 × 1 cm). Wrap it around one end of a stem wire, cover the paper towel with a strip of paper that has been stretched and coated with craft glue, then add a few sepals.

Flower Hair Clips

- Materials -

Scrapbooking paper, 230 gr:
violet, white

Flower paper punch | Extra-strength glue
1 set of bobby pins with round blank

1

Using a flower-shaped hole punch, punch flower shapes from the paper. To make one raised flower, you will need five identical shapes.

2

With your fingers, fold each petal in half to give them movement.

Take one flower and form a flower bud by applying a few dots of extra-strength glue and folding the petals inward. Glue the bud to the center of a second flower, then fold over and glue the petals to the bud.

Place three flowers on top of each other, gluing them together in the center, then attach your bud to the center. Using your fingers, reshape the flower by folding the petals toward the middle.

Secure the flower to the round blank on your bobby pin using extra-strength glue.

TIP

Vary the flower shapes with different flower punches. Create a set of small blooms and buds to embellish your hair for a special occasion.

Pansy Ring

Pansy Ring

- Materials -

Crepe paper: white

Scissors | Hot glue gun | White craft glue
Foam brush | Thin artist's brush | Watercolors
Felt-tip pen | 1 flat ring blank

1

For this tutorial, first laminate the paper (see page 15). For this pattern, you will need a thickness of two sheets of crepe paper. Once the paper is completely dry, cut out five petals using the templates on page 95: two A, two B, and one C.

2

Choose the color of pansy you want to create and replicate the shading on the petals. The more you dilute the watercolor, the lighter the hue. Layer to create darker shades, allowing the paint to dry between coats.

3

You can finish off the coloring by drawing fine lines with a felt-tip pen for added detail or watercolor with a very fine brush.

4

Attach the two B petals to the back of the C petal with a dot of hot glue, then the two A petals behind the B petals. You may choose to place a decorative ornament in the center of the pansy. Finally, attach the pansy to the flat blank of the ring with a dot of hot glue.

INSPIRATION

Here are four ideas for coloring to help create the look of a pansy:

Back *Jewelry*

- *Materials* -

Crepe paper or tissue paper: white

Scissors | Needle-nose pliers | Round-nose pliers | Wire cutters

Extra-strength glue or hot glue gun | 3 jump rings

1 mother-of-pearl teardrop pendant | 1 decorative charm | Fine-link chain

1

With a wire cutter, cut a 10" (25 cm) length of chain. Open a jump ring with the flat-nose and round-nose pliers, add the mother-of-pearl teardrop to the ring and, before closing it, add one end of your chain to the ring.

2

Using the template on page 95, cut out eight flowers. Fold one in half, then in half again, giving some dimension to your flower. Do this four times. Then glue the last four flowers one on top of the other to form a little flower with several petals.

3

About 4" (10 cm) above the mother-of-pearl teardrop, glue two of the folded flowers back to back, around the chain, using hot glue or extra-strength glue, then again glue two of the folded flowers back to back, in the same way, 4" (10 cm) from the first one so that the decorative chain hangs down the back.

4

With the wire cutters, cut two lengths of chain about 12" (30 cm) long. With the flat-nose and round-nose pliers, open a jump ring, and add the two ends of your two lengths of chain as well as your decorative charm.

5

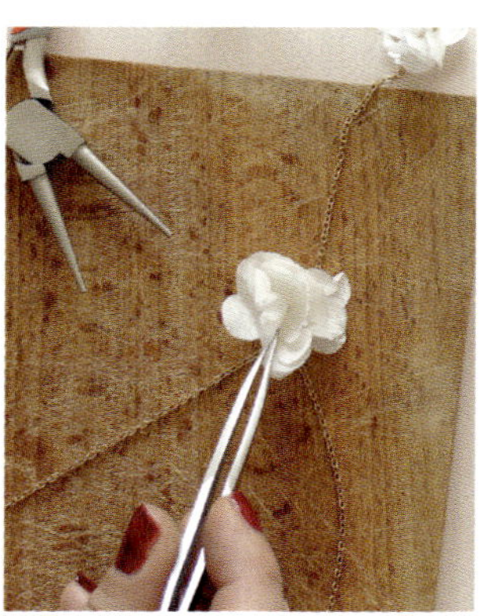

Put a drop of extra-strength glue or hot glue on the jump ring and glue it to the flower with the many petals. I use a jump ring so that the flower will lie flat against the back.

6

To finish this piece of jewelry for the back, open a jump ring with the flat-nose and round-nose pliers, add the two lengths of chain that will form your necklace and the decorative charm that will be at the front of your neck before closing the ring.

TIP

If you don't have anything to wear with an open back, try a V-neck vest that you can wear backward!

Cherry Blossom Earrings

Cherry Blossom *Earrings*

- *Materials* -

Crepe paper: white

Scissors | Needle-nose pliers | Round-nose pliers | White craft glue
Hot glue gun | Floral tape | Artificial stamens
Thin aluminum wire | PanPastels (optional) | 2 jump rings
2 teardrop hoops | 2 fishhook ear wires

1

Using the template on page 95, cut out the desired number of petals for your earrings. You will need five petals for each cherry blossom. Stretch your paper slightly beforehand to soften the grain of the paper.

2

To make it look more realistic, you can add shades of color to your petals with PanPastels, watercolors, felt-tip pens, etc. Here, I'm coloring the petals slightly to give them a pinkish hue and adding some red to the bottom of the petals using PanPastels.

3

Using floral tape or a strip of paper previously stretched and coated with craft glue, attach the artificial stamens to a thin aluminum wire.

4

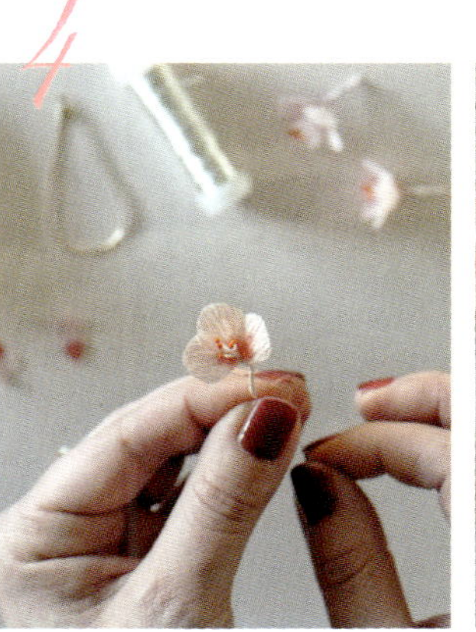

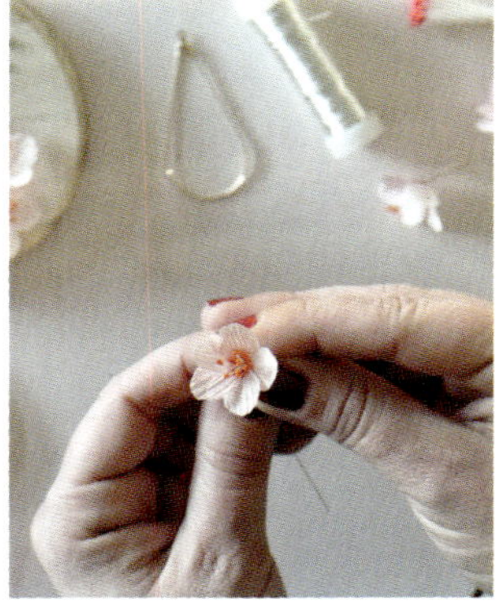

Glue the five petals one after the other around the stamens. Cherry blossom stamens are fairly long and should be positioned at the same height as the petals.

5

Cover the aluminum wire starting from the calyx of the flower with floral tape or a strip of paper previously stretched and coated with craft glue. Twist this wire around the teardrop hoop and use it as a base for your other flowers.

6

Cut the thin aluminum wire below the calyx of the cherry blossoms, then secure them with a dot of hot glue.

7

Open a jump ring using round-nose and flat-nose pliers. Thread on the teardrop hoop with the flowers and a fishhook ear wire, then close the ring.

Floral *Headband*

- Materials -

Crepe paper: gold

Scissors | White craft glue | Thin aluminum wire

Needle | Mother-of-pearl beads | 1 headband base

1

Make flowers of different sizes. To do this, fold a square in four and cut out a flower outline imagining the center of the flower in the folded corner.

2

Cover the headband with a ⅜" (1 cm)–wide strip of stretched paper coated with white craft glue.

3

Make a hole in the center of the flowers with a needle.

4

Thread one bead onto a length of thin aluminum wire, placing it in the center of the wire. Give the wire a twist right under the bead to lock it in place. Then pass the two aluminum wires through the hole in a flower, putting the bead at the center of it.

- Assembly -

Position the flowers around the headband starting on one side and trim off any excess aluminum wire. Let your own creativity inspire the placement of the flowers, playing around with the different sizes and shapes.

Inspiring Collaborations

Candice Aubert-Dhô

Textile artist Candice Aubert-Dhô opened her studio in Provence because she believes it is possible to change tomorrow's world by starting with ourselves.

Everything she makes is created with a committed, ethically based approach. All the materials she uses are handcrafted, French, natural, and/or recycled and reclaimed, prioritizing her local French artisanal supply channels that respect our environment, for both humans and animals.

Merino wool from Arles, handmade ceramics, French rope, fabric from T-shirts, natural dyes, etc. Each creation is the sum of many skills found in France.

This authentic approach inspires her and enables her to create many meaningful items.

You can find her work at:
www.cosyjungle.fr
Instagram : @_cosyjungle_

- WITH -

Candice Aubert-Dhô
from Cosy Jungle

- Materials -

Crepe paper: white, pink

¼" (0.5 cm) wired cotton for the warp or a very thin twine

5½ to 11 yards (5 to 10 m) of various yarns and cords in your choice of colors

Scissors | Weaving needle (with a large eye) | Artificial stamens

Foam brush | White craft glue | Hot glue gun

1 bag made of natural materials (rope, jute, wicker, caning, etc.)

1

To help you get your bearings while weaving, make a paper pattern to guide you. On a sheet of paper, draw the shape you'd like to reproduce. Cut it out and place it in the desired position on your bag.

A SUGGESTION FROM CANDICE

Before you start weaving, select your yarns and cut them in different lengths! Your weave will create itself when you alternate them, and you'll be sure to end up with a unique creation.

2

Create the warp

You'll need to create a warp through which to weave your weft. Following the pattern outline, make a tight double knot with the warp thread on the lower left-hand side of your shape. Pull the thread tight to the opposite edge and stitch into the bag. Bring the thread back down and stitch about ⅜" (1 cm) to the right of the starting point. Continue stitching into the bag at the top and bottom edges of the shape.

3

Finish attaching the warp

Once your pattern has been reproduced on the bag, check the thread tension. If it is too loose, go ahead and tighten the threads (without distorting your bag). Finally, make a double knot to secure the thread. Remove the pattern. You can now start weaving.

4

Start weaving

To weave, start at the bottom of your shape. Pass the yarn over one warp thread then under the next. Continue repeating this "over/under" step until the entire shape is filled. Let your own inspiration guide you as you weave!

Be sure to press your rows of yarn down frequently. Let at least ⅜" (1 cm) of yarn hang out on the reverse side when one thread ends and do the same for the first and last yarns woven.

To change yarn: Let yarn A end on the wrong side, then bring yarn B up from the back side right where you left off. Any gap between the two yarns will be masked by the next row of yarn. Press down well to pack the rows together.

5

Finish weaving

Fill the shape by weaving right up to the edges. **Alternate yarns and materials:** Allow yourself this time to simply create and make your own totally unique bag. Once your warp yarn has been filled, tuck in any protruding threads toward the back side to hide them.

- The Flowers -

1

For this tutorial, first follow the steps to laminate the paper (see page 15). To make the little flowers, you'll need a thickness of four sheets of crepe paper.

2

Using the template on page 95, cut out the petals needed for the number of flowers you wish to add to your woven bag.

3

Gather three or four artificial stamens in the center of a petal, secure with a dot of hot glue, then glue as many petals as you'd like around this first petal to create your little flowers. You can make small flowers with three petals and others with six petals.

4

Place a dot of hot glue where you would like your blooms to be on the bag, then attach your little flowers for a lovely finish.

Feel free to create your own template for larger or smaller flowers to suit your style! Your woven bag can be used on your everyday spring outings but also as a decoration for your home. Hung on the wall on a pretty peg, it's the ideal container for your magazines or a pretty bouquet of long-lasting paper flowers.

Inspiring Collaborations

Sandrina Rocha

Sandrina Rocha founded her eponymous brand in 2016 with a strong environmental focus.

The artist specializes in creating pieces of high-end art, decor, and fashion, all in harmony with nature.

Each piece is a unique work of art, entirely handmade in Sandrina's Lyon workshop. From dyeing to couture, each step is carried out with care and attention to detail.

One of this eco-responsible brand's distinguishing features is the use of artisanal dyeing processes. These techniques give each piece a unique and singular appearance. Sandrina uses a variety of organic materials, minerals, nontoxic metals, and even food waste to create her colors and patterns.

You can find her work at:
www.sandrinarocha.com
Instagram : @sandrina__rocha

- WITH -

Sandrina Rocha
from Woola La!

- Materials -

For the ribbon:
4" x 17" (10 x 42 cm) piece of silk (including ⅜" (1 cm) seam allowance)
Yellow onion peel | White vinegar | String or rubber bands | Pinking shears
Steamer basket and pot
Sewing machine or thread and needle for hand sewing

For the sustainable peony:
Crepe paper: pale pink, soft yellow, green
Scissors | Wire cutters | Hot glue gun | White craft glue
Yellow felt-tip pen | Stem wire | Paper towel | PanPastels (optional)
1 cuff bracelet blank

1

What to know before starting

As a general rule, utensils used for dyeing are no longer usable for cooking, but here, onion peels are nontoxic, so there's no risk to you!

Normally before dyeing, you would prepare natural fiber to receive dye by mordanting with alum, a step that helps to fix the color. Alum is used at a rate of 20 percent of the weight of the fiber to be dyed. However, silk is a protein fiber that binds wonderfully well to natural dyes, so you can skip this step for this project.

2

Eco-print dyeing

The pattern is created when the peel touches the fabric. Soak the silk fabric in a mixture of water and white vinegar until it is thoroughly saturated. Spread out the piece of silk. Cut the peelings into small pieces and arrange them as desired on the fabric. Then roll up the fabric tightly and hold closed with string or rubber bands. Place the package in a basket over a saucepan of simmering water and steam for one hour, covered. Then wash the fabric with a pH-neutral soap, rinse with clean water, wring out, and iron damp.

3

Sewing

Fold the piece of silk in half lengthwise, right sides together. Sew the three sides together by machine or by hand, ⅜" (1 cm) from the edge, leaving an opening about 2" (5 cm) long on the longest side for turning. Trim excess fabric from edges using pinking shears. Iron the seams open for a more attractive finish and turn the bracelet right sides to the outside. Use a chopstick or something similar to push out the corners. Iron the ribbon and close the remaining opening with an invisible seam.

– The Sustainable Peony –

1

Stretch strips of crepe paper to the size of the petal template on page 95 until you feel a slight tension. Then cut out twenty-five petals using the template, making sure that the grain of the paper is vertical when cutting (the same direction as the two lines on the template).

2

Cut a strip of yellow paper to 4" x 1" (10 x 2.5 cm) and stretch it until you feel a slight tension.
Along its entire length, color the edge of the paper with a yellow felt-tip pen to represent the stamens' anthers.

Then fold the strip in half and in half again and cut a fringe as fine as possible, leaving a ¼" (0.5 cm) edge uncut, which you'll use to glue your petals.

3

Form a ball from a strip of paper towel 4" long x ⅝" wide (10 x 1.5 cm) and attach it to one end of the stem wire. To do this, open the ball slightly, apply a dot of hot glue, slide your stem inside, then round it with your fingers.

Cut a ¾" x 1¼" (2 × 3 cm) piece of stretched green paper, coat it with white craft glue, position the stem wire in the center, and cover the ball to form the peony's pistil.

4

Secure one end of your stamen strip to the stem wire under the pistil with hot glue, apply craft glue to the uncut part, then roll it up completely. Apply some tension to make sure it is wrapped tightly and is kept at the same position on the stem. For extra hold, apply hot glue to the base of the strip once it is fully wound.

5

You can tint the top of the petals with a PanPastel to add depth to your peony. If necessary, you can use a makeup palette.

To curve your petals, smooth each petal with your fingers and nails.

6

Glue petals to the edges of your cuff blank to visually cover it.

7

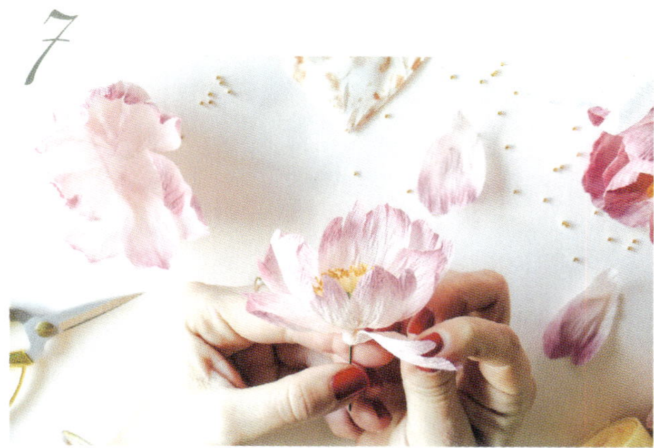

Glue the rest of the petals onto the uncut base of the strip of stamens you've just wound onto the stem, letting your inspiration guide the placement, so that the result is aesthetically pleasing and to your liking. You can overlap them or place them side by side. To finish, cut the stem wire with wire cutters, apply hot glue to the center of the cuff blank, and glue on your peony.

All that's left is to add your naturally dyed ribbon to the cuff blank.

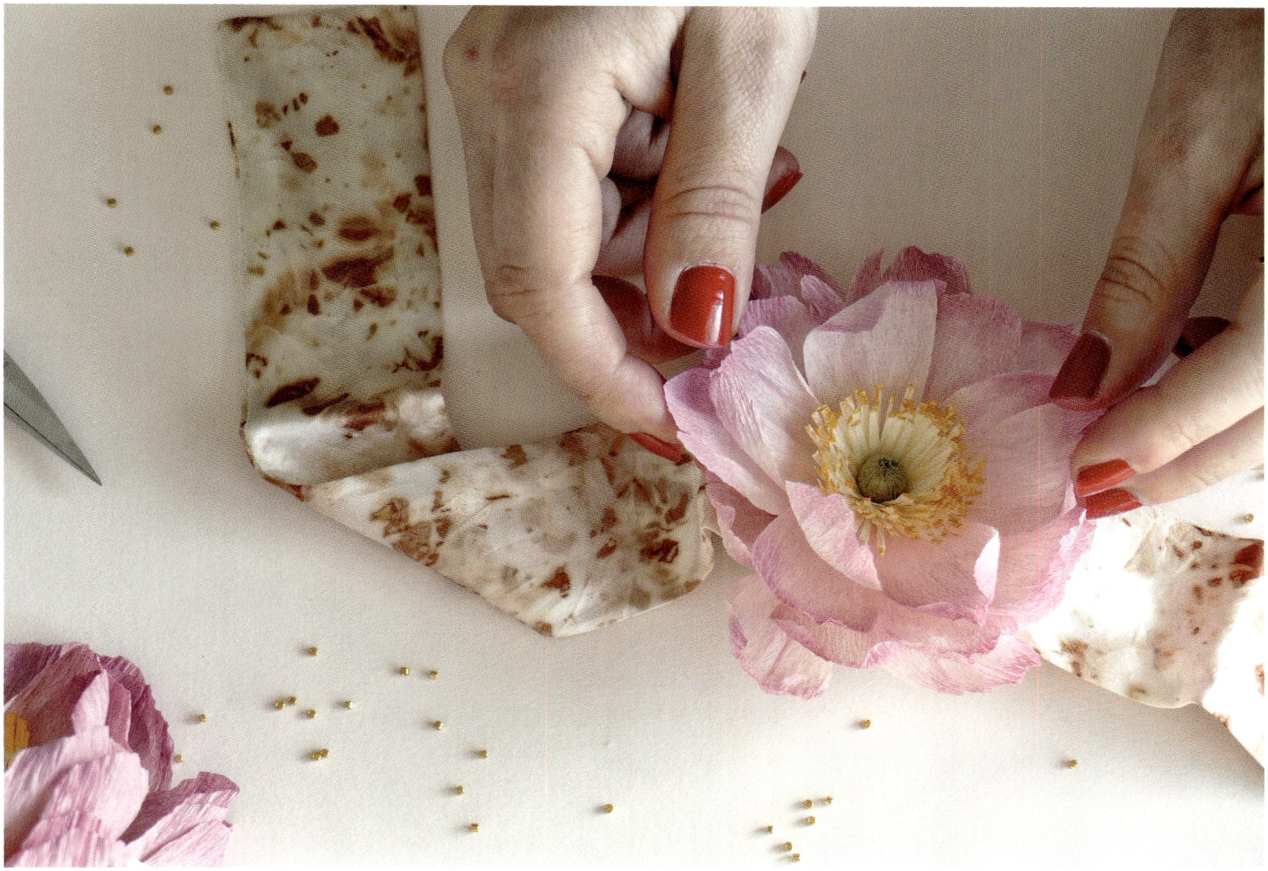

A WORD FROM THE AUTHOR

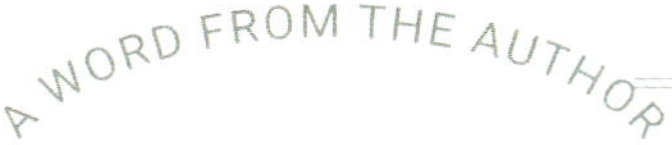

A bit vintage, the floral cuff brings to mind the timeless charm of a bygone era, and is a beautiful accessory to add a romantic touch on a special occasion such as a wedding.

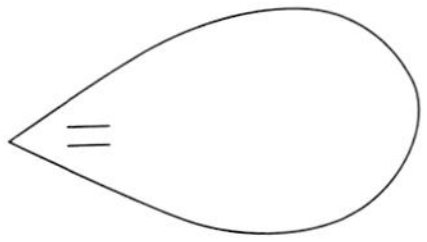

Half Flower Lever-Back Earrings

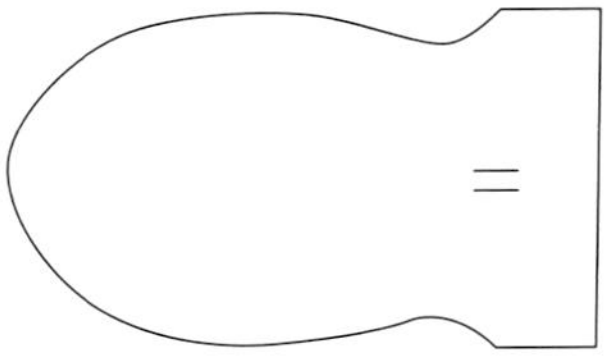

Carnation Pin

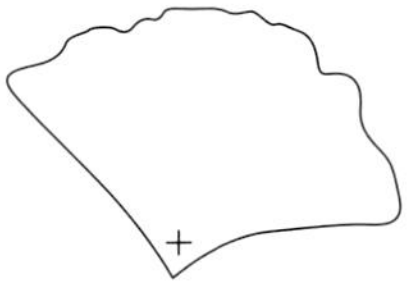

Ginkgo Dangle Earrings

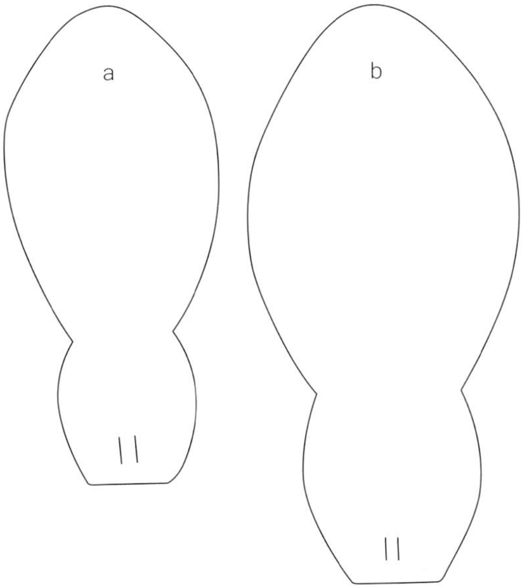

a

b

Magnolia Hairpins

Flower Pin

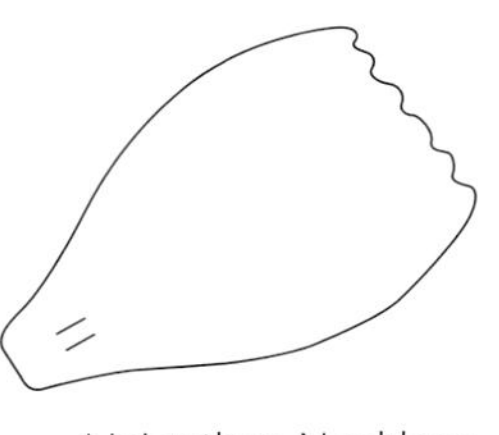

Lisianthus Necklace

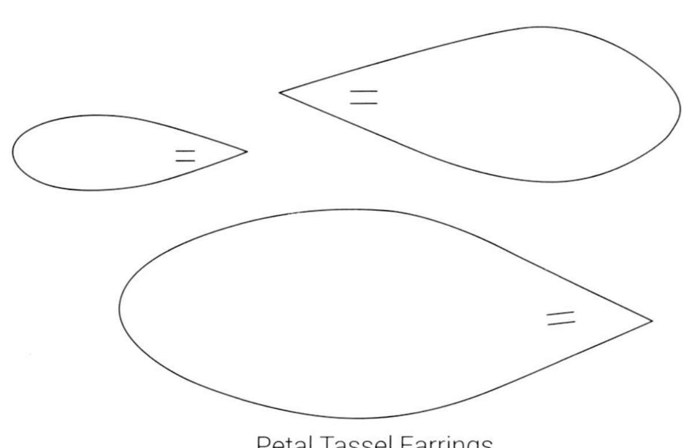

Petal Tassel Earrings

Energizing Ring

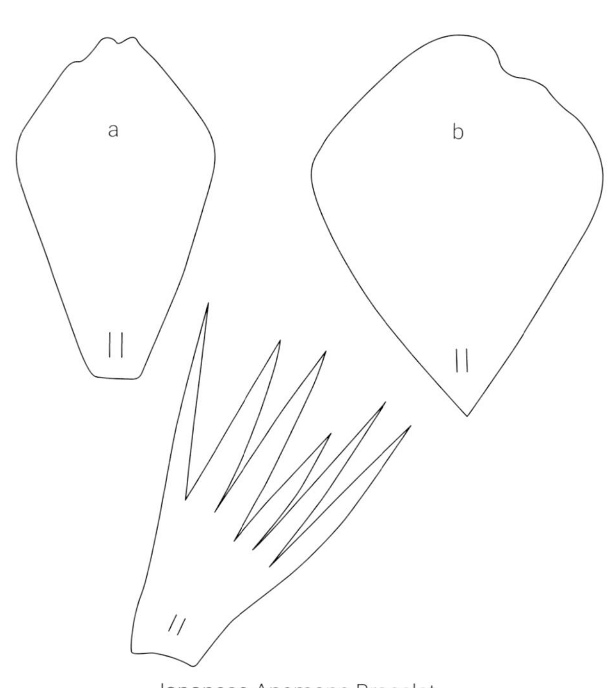

Japanese Anemone Bracelet

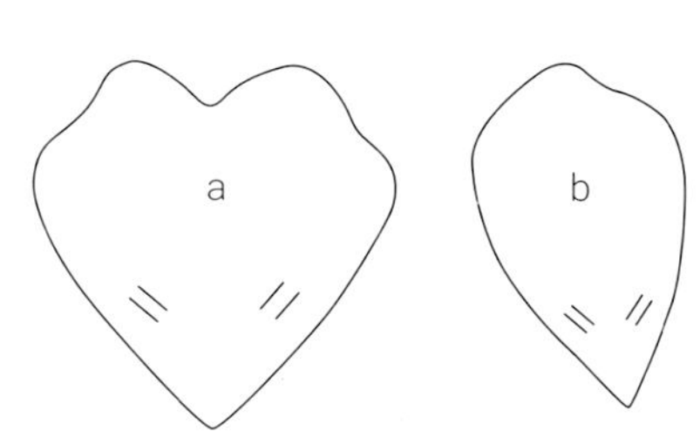

Sweet Pea Hair Comb

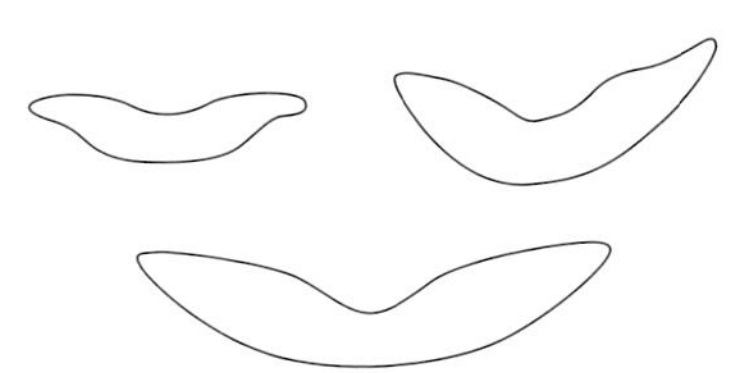

Gold Leaf Hoop Earrings

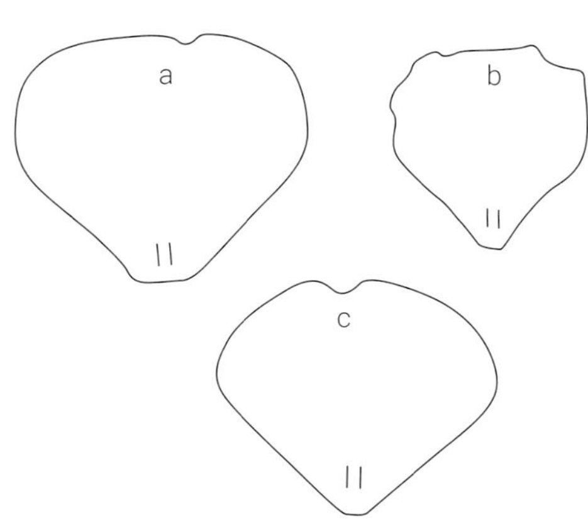

Pansy Ring

Back Jewelry

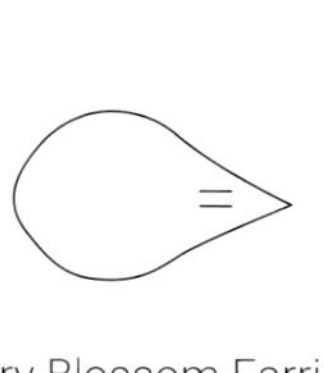

Cherry Blossom Earrings

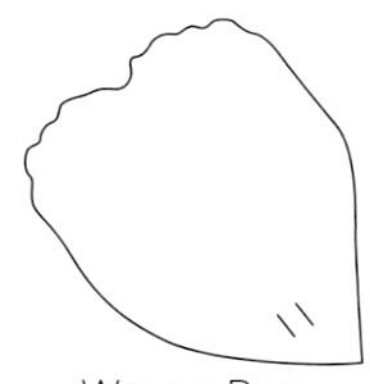

Woven Bag

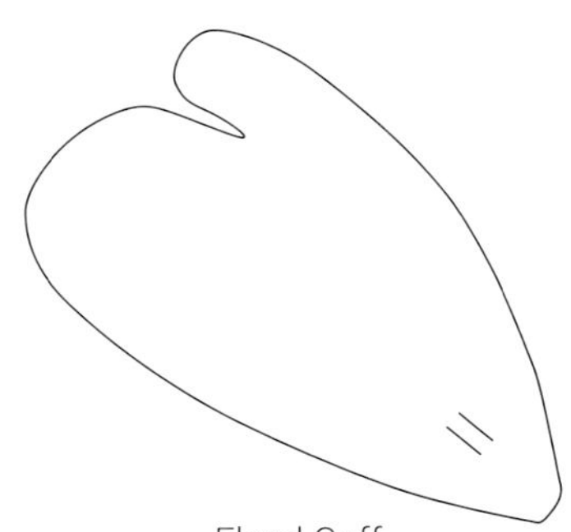

Floral Cuff

STACKPOLE BOOKS
An imprint of The Globe Pequot Publishing Group, Inc.
64 South Main Street
Essex, CT 06426
www.GlobePequot.com

Author: Laura Flavigny

Projects: Laura Flavigny
Photos and Styling: Candice Aubert-Dhô, Sandrina Rocha, Kathryn M of Sages comme des images, Anne-Sophie Annese of Studio Bohème, Solenne Jakovsky, Rachel Saddedine
Models: Camille Dudreuil, Mila Valero-Flavigny
Text: Laura Flavigny
Layout and Illustrations: Christine Lim
Technical Drawing: Céline Cantat

British Library Cataloguing in Publication Information available

Library of Congress Cataloging-in-Publication Data available
ISBN 978-0-8117-7709-4 (paper : alk. paper)
ISBN 978-0-8117-7710-0 (electronic)

Printed in India